HoC

D1384576

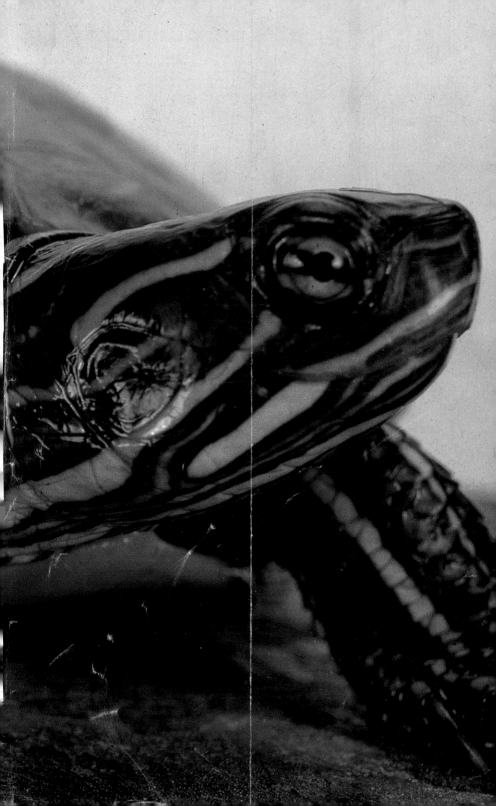

a

Turtles

John M. Mehrtens

Distributed in the UNITED STATES by T.F.H. Publications, Inc., 211 West
Sylvania Avenue, Neptune City, NJ 07753; in CANADA by H & L Pet Supplies
Inc., 27 Kingston Crescent, Kitchener, Ontario N2B 2T6; Rolf C. Hagen Ltd.,
3225 Sartelon Street, Montreal 382 Quebec; in ENGLAND by T.F.H. Publica-
tions Limited, 4 Kier Park, Ascot, Berkshire SL5 7DS; in AUSTRALIA AND
THE SOUTH PACIFIC by T.F.H. (Australia) Pty. Ltd., Box 149, Brookvale
2100 N.S.W., Australia; in NEW ZEALAND by Ross Haines & Son, Ltd., 18
Monmouth Street, Grey Lynn, Auckland 2 New Zealand; in SINGAPORE
AND MALAYSIA by MPH Distributors (S) Pte., Ltd., 601 Sims Drive,
03/07/21, Singapore 1438; in the PHILIPPINES by Bio-Research, 5 Lippay
Street, San Lorenzo Village, Makati Rizal; in SOUTH AFRICA by Multipet
Pty. Ltd., 30 Turners Avenue, Durban 4001. Published by T.F.H. Publications
Inc., Ltd. the British Crown Colony of Hong Kong.

Contents

Posters

A: Close-up of the northern painted turtle, *Chrysemys picta picta*. Photo by Dr. Herbert R. Axelrod.

B: A small South African tortoise, *Homopus areolatus*. Photo by Dr. Herbert R. Axelrod.

C: A large *Podocnemis expansa* collected by a Brazilian Indian for food. Photo by Harald Schultz.

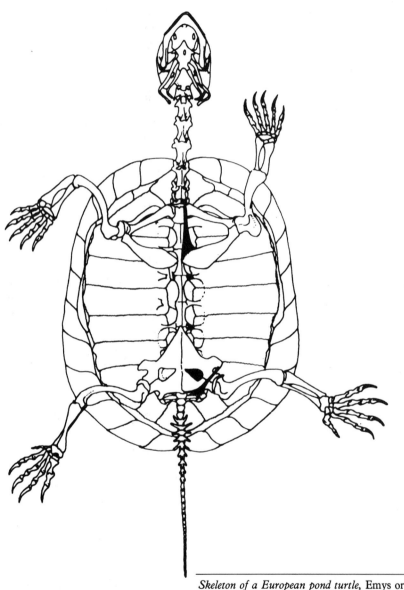

Skeleton of a European pond turtle, Emys orbicularis. *The plastron (undershell) has been removed to show the skeleton from underneath.*

Introduction

Why keep turtles? Certainly you will be enjoying a pet that has been kept by many of the famous personalities of history. Relatively simple to care for, many species are as colorful as tropical fishes. Further, they are not nearly as demanding as mammalian pets (dogs, cats, etc.), yet are remarkably responsive to their owners—and, in addition, are silent! Compressed in their rigid shells and lacking agility and expression, turtles are often considered not too bright, except by those who know them best. Turtles learn to know their owners; they appreciate gentle care; and they can be taught simple responses.

Not enough? Then tell your friends you keep a prehistoric creature as a pet. Certainly they'll be relieved to find it is a harmless turtle or tortoise instead of a dinosaur. But you are not guilty of exaggeration, for they are truly "living fossils," essentially unchanged for over a hundred million years.

This book is not only about turtles, but also about how to care for them; it's easy when you know how. Turtles are in the home to stay. It is the purpose of this book to acquaint the reader with the facts and fallacies of turtle keeping. Whether kept as an adult hobby or as a child's pet, turtles are living things and as such should be kept under conditions conducive to their health and well-being.

What is a turtle?

Turtles are reptiles—so-called cold-blooded animals related to but distinct from the snakes, lizards, and crocodiles, all also reptiles. Technically, they form the reptilian order (group) Chelonia.

Turtles had developed their protective shells long before the dinosaurs appeared. Once ensconced in their protective shells, the turtles became ultra-conservative. Although they inhabited many environments, the basic blueprint never changed. The group, as did other reptiles, produced its giants, such as *Geochelone sivalensis*, a tortoise from India that had a shell 6 feet long, and *Archelon*, a giant marine turtle with a shell 8 feet long. Today, millions of years later, turtles range in size from the leatherback (*Dermochelys*), which has a 6-foot shell and weighs 1300 pounds, to a diminutive mud turtle that matures at 3 inches.

Physical characteristics

The turtle's outstanding physical

Introduction

feature, its shell, is formed of elongated and hardened plates of bone. These plates represent a specialized modification of the ribs and vertebral processes. The plates are covered with semi-transparent overlapping *scutes* made of a hornlike substance similar to the scales of a snake or lizard. The upper shell is called the *carapace,* and the lower shell the *plastron.*

The soft-shell turtles have the underlying plates covered with skin rather than scutes.

Turtles have no teeth, the jaws usually being equipped with rather sharp shearing edges or broad crushing surfaces. In some species, a combination of the two is found, and in others it is completely lacking, as in the matamata. Technically this structure is called the *tomium.*

Being reptiles and unable to regulate their internal temperature (poikilothermic), turtles rely heavily on the environment to provide the body heat necessary for metabolism. Thus, at low temperatures they refuse to feed, and in the wild they will hibernate until spring warmth allows them to function again. Too much heat is also dangerous, and many desert forms sleep away the hottest months in a cool burrow (estivation).

With but few exceptions, turtles have excellent eyesight; some species, at least, recognize color. All turtles have a well-developed sense of hearing, although they do not have external ears. They reproduce by laying eggs in a nest dug in sandy soil by the female. Incubated by the solar heat, the eggs hatch in five to ten weeks, the youngsters digging out of the nest and entering the water immediately. There is no parental care. Some northern species hatch in the fall but remain in the nest until the following spring, surviving on the remains of the egg yolk. Baby turtles break their way out of the egg shell with an "egg tooth," a small structure located on the snout. Most other reptiles, as well as birds, share this structure and use it to break out of their shells.

Generally, most aquatic turtles are *carnivores*, feeding on the flesh of various animals. Terrestrial (land-dwelling) forms, such as the tortoises, are *herbivores*, feeding on plants. However, food preferences are often reversed or intermixed. Thus, with the exception of a few specialized forms, the group as a whole is here considered *omnivorous*, eating both plant and animal matter.

There are approximately 350 species and subspecies (forms and

Introduction

varieties) of chelonians living today. They are almost restricted to the temperate and tropical regions of the earth and reach their greatest abundance in the latter.

Turtles and man

Turtles have evoked the curiosity and interest, both culinary and esthetic, of man for ages. Unfortunately, when man takes an interest in a fellow creature, it often winds up dead. Probably the most outstanding contribution the turtle has made to man is as food. The giant tortoises of the Galapagos and Seychelle Islands are today faced with extinction because of their use as food aboard sailing ships. Kept alive for months without food or water, the tortoises provided fresh meat for the sailors in the days when ocean voyages lasted for months or years. Often a thousand or more would be taken by one or two ships. Sea turtles, especially the green turtle (*Chelonia mydas*), are used for turtle steaks and soups, and in addition, the eggs of all sea turtles still are collected by the thousands and sold as food. Freshwater species are not exempt from such decimation, especially in tropical countries where both eggs and

adults (usually female) are eaten. Some control now exists, but it is doubtful that it will do more than temporarily slow the extirpation. "Tortoise shell," especially popular in the nineteenth century for combs, jewelry, and cabinet work, comes from the scutes of the hawksbill turtle (*Eretmochelys imbricata*), a marine species . The living turtles were peeled of their scutes by being suspended over a fire until the scutes curled off the underlying bone. The hapless turtle was then returned to the sea with the idea that it would regrow the plates. Actually, it died a lingering death.

The Chinese so esteem the flesh of the indigenous species of soft-shell turtle that they have introduced it into all areas where they have settled. As a result of this, the animal today has a most unusual distribution, including California and Hawaii.

Vast numbers of the small geometric and rayed tortoises of southern Africa (*Psammobates*) had their colorful shells converted into souvenir jewel and snuff boxes. The practice has been stopped by the government, but both species are considered rarities today.

Centuries ago, the various tribes in the Aegean area used the flared shells of the margined tortoise

Introduction

(*Testudo marginata*) as helmets. The shell of this species and its cousin, the Greek tortoise (*T. graeca*), were also used as sound boxes for lutes and lyres. The giant leatherback turtle mentioned earlier is often called a "luth," the word deriving from the same root word as "lute." The word "lyre" derives from the ancient Greek word for turtle, "lyra." Incidentally, American Indians used the shell of the box turtle as a rattle for ceremonial dancing. Thousands of adult turtles (usually *Pseudemys*) are dissected by students in biology every year. Many more are used in parasitological work. Millions of hatchlings were once sold each year as pets.

On the other hand, man has often venerated turtles. The Orientals consider it the symbol of long life, a likeness of the animal often appearing with an appropriate god. A few primitive tribes consider their local turtles to be soul repositories for their ancestors and feed and revere them. A Hindu myth had the world carried on the back of a giant tortoise, while Arabian astronomers gave the name of the turtle to a constellation. And, of course, the turtle has served man as a natural symbol of perseverance: everyone recalls how the tortoise won the race from the hare, as Aesop wrote in the fable.

Longevity

There is a great deal of popular interest in the life span of certain animals, especially, it seems, parrots, turtles, and alligators. Sunday magazines report with some regularity about 300-year-old reptiles and five-generation parrots. While some animals are quite long-lived by human standards, most such stories are exaggerations. In the wild, all animals are subject to many dangers, so (with some exceptions, of course) records of extreme longevity are usually based on captive animals with a known history.

Little credence can be attached to turtles with dates carved into their shells, for this is an obviously easy means of fakery, especially since most turtles so dated also carry the name of a famous personage of the time. One exception to this concerns an eastern box turtle (*Terrapene c. carolina*) that was kept as a pet by succeeding generations of a single family. The family's history of this turtle, along with the carved date 1839, has proven the age of the animal to be in excess of 140 years.

Introduction

"Marion's tortoise," an Aldabara giant tortoise, was collected from the Seychelle Islands in 1776 and kept as a pet at a French settlement on Mauritius. Mauritius was captured by the British, at which time the tortoise was considered a prize of war and formally turned over to the British by the defeated French. The tortoise eventually went blind but continued to be the pet of the British garrison until it died in a fall in 1918. Since the tortoise was adult at capture in 1776, it was at least 25 years old at that time. Its captive history covers 142 years, thus giving it a life span of about 167 years—venerable old age indeed!

"Teddy" Roosevelt returned from the Amazonian "River of Doubt" Expedition in 1914. He brought with him a pet red-legged tortoise (*Geochelone carbonaria*). This animal, adult when collected, lived a long life at the Bronx Zoo in New York, reaching at least 85 years old. As might be expected, it was named Teddy.

Many records exist of captives living from 25 to 50 years, this age probably representing the usual longevity for the smaller aquatic forms. Little is known about maximum age in the wild. Several species are now the subject of field marking work, but such research has not been conducted long enough yet to provide accurate data.

Summing up, most of the smaller aquatic turtles can survive for at least 50 years. Tortoises probably live somewhat longer, about 75 years. A few larger species, such as giant tortoises and probably sea turtles, appear capable of surviving for a century.

Intelligence

If one considers that turtles have kept the same basic model and style for millions of years and have managed in that time to exploit many varied habitats successfully, then indeed it must be a very "intelligent critter." On the other hand, if we choose to compare turtle brain power with that of a dog or a monkey, we must say that the turtle is certainly not very bright. However, this is an unfair comparison. Let us just say that turtles have whatever "intelligence" they need to survive, and this is enough, also, to make them engaging and responsive pets.

Training

Turtles learn most quickly through

Introduction

association. For instance, gently tapping one corner of their living quarters just before feeding will shortly induce the animals to come to this corner immediately *whenever* it is tapped. But remember, the conditioning process must be consistent and, initially at least, should take place at the same time each day. The obvious next step is to induce the animal to feed from the fingers. Slow at first, they soon associate tapping, food, and fingers. Once confidence is established, aquatic turtles will literally swim on their backs with necks outstretched for food.

Turtles and tortoises will often teach themselves "tricks." I know of an adult gopher tortoise (*Gopherus polyphemus*) named Samson who goes to the refrigerator at the proper time and waits for his ration. A wood turtle (*Clemmys insculpta*) when hungry would seek out his owner and stand on his foot. If nothing was forthcoming, the animal wagged one of its forelegs. It should be explained, however, that the owner fixed this trait by feeding the animal only after it had gone through the routine.

Turtles have an excellent sense of timing. If they are fed at the same time and place each day, they will soon learn to proceed to the proper place at the proper time, each and every day. However, if you feed them only six days a week, they will never learn to skip the seventh day. Apparently their time sense is based on a 24-hour rhythm.

Some turtles, especially wood turtles and spotted turtles (*Clemmys guttata*), and tortoises will learn to walk simple mazes for a food reward. It is informative and entertaining to construct simple mazes and to keep notes on the time involved in learning them. Comparisons can be made between your specimens, other species of turtles, and even rats and mice. Any large library has books available which deal with this subject in detail.

Personality

All animals have "personalities" that make them distinguishable from their fellows. Any person caring for a large number of similar specimens readily distinguishes individuals on the basis of temperament, individual idiosyncrasies, and habitual actions. A friend in Scotland keeps a pair of Hermann's tortoises (*Testudo hermanni*) in her garden and at a distance can readily tell Fred, the male, from Frederika, the female.

10

Selecting a Turtle

Each specimen exhibits distinctive personality traits recognized by its owner. Incidentally, these tortoises come to their owner when called by name.

Success in keeping large collections of turtles, and other animals for that matter, depends to some degree on recognizing their "personality" traits. An aggressive specimen, perfectly capable of looking after itself, will often overshadow and hog the care and attention that might better go to its more shy and retiring cousin that really does require careful personal consideration.

Teaching a pet turtle a few "tricks" is good for the animal and certainly makes the pet more attractive to its owner. Simple notes are easily kept, and quite often the owner learns something himself. It should be noted here that turtles have no concept of punishment in the usual sense of the word: It should also be noted that no animal is going to respond to "training" unless it is in good health and kept under proper physical conditions.

Although most pet turtles sold once were hatchlings, local and state health regulations now largely prohibit the sale of turtles under 3 or 4 inches long. Unless even these relatively large turtles receive proper care, they will be difficult to raise to maturity or, for that matter, even to keep alive for a few months. The survival of a pet turtle depends to a large extent upon the treatment it has received before it is purchased. Therefore, attention should be paid to the conditions under which the turtles are kept by the dealer. Inasmuch as proper housing is a simple matter, the dealer should take care to provide it.

Clean, fresh water must be available at all times, for water turtles cannot swallow food unless submerged. An electric light bulb or other source of heat should be evident, unless the store is always kept warm. A turtle badly chilled for days in an air-conditioned shop environment runs the risk of either pneumonia or gastric disturbances. The stock tank should provide a rock island or other suitable basking site, preferably under a lamp. As previously stated, turtles are *living* creatures and should not be treated like so many potatoes.

Mention should be made here of the practice of painting the shells of

Selecting a Turtle

juvenile turtles with landscape scenes, sayings, and flowers. The shell of a turtle is a living, growing part of the animal, and such a practice prevents the shell from growing normally. Indeed, if the turtle should manage to survive, the painted shell becomes so misshapen that the turtle cannot breathe and soon dies. In the event that you do become the owner of a turtle that has an enamelled shell, the paint should be gently flaked off as soon as possible. The shells of most juvenile turtles are so attractively colored and patterned to begin with that painting detracts from rather than enhances their appearance.

DO'S AND DON'TS OF TURTLE BUYING

1. **Avoid** a turtle with a soft shell. The rear marginals especially should be firm to the touch. While the condition is reversible, this requires special care and attention. Needless to say, this does not apply to soft-shell turtles (*Trionyx*).
2. **Do not** buy a turtle that has swollen, puffy eyes.
3. **Do not** buy legally protected species.
4. **Do** remove the paint from turtles with painted shells.
5. **Do not** buy a turtle that you cannot properly house and care for.
6. **Do** buy turtles that are bright eyed and able to swim actively.
7. **Do** buy turtles that either vigorously retract head and legs when picked up or vigorously "swim" in the air.

Collecting turtles in the wild

Turtles are difficult to collect without some knowledge of their habits in the area where you live. Consult one of the many field guides available at libraries and book stores for this information. According to the number of specimens or the species desired, turtles may be hand collected, either while they are swimming or moving about on land, netted, or trapped. A variety of traps is available commercially, and several types are easily constructed out of scrap materials. Juveniles may be collected at night by shining a bright light on submerged brushpiles, where they often sleep.

At certain times turtles are found wandering across highways, often in considerable numbers. These, of course, may

Food and Water

simply be picked up. Box turtles, sliders, mud turtles, snappers, and tortoises are commonly found in this manner.

If you do collect your own specimens, take only those that you can properly care for. Turtles that have been captured locally and are no longer wanted should be released where they were found. **Do not** release specimens from other areas into local waters. Such specimens should be given to a local zoo or similar institution.

Do not keep legally protected species. Many states have laws against capturing wild animals and keeping them as pets. I suggest that you write to the State Department of Conservation in your state capital or get in touch with your local humane society for the laws and regulations applicable in your area.

Some creatures may be fed adequately just by opening a can; that is not true for turtles. The small containers of turtle food sold commercially are intended for aquatics only. Although some (notably pelleted food) are superior to others, all of them should be supplemented. Feed the commercial pellet types a few at a time and make sure that the turtle clears them up, as uneaten excess may foul the tank. Dried "flies" (really water insects) and "ant eggs" (really not eggs, but ant pupae) are deficient in protein, fats, and digestible carbohydrates, as well as certain other nutrients.

Temperature

Turtles can only eat and digest food when they are kept at the proper temperature. Most turtles are comfortable at a temperature of 75 to 85°F, although a drop to as low as 65°F overnight will do no harm. Desert tortoises will tolerate temperatures as high as 90°F for short periods.

A turtle shows its distress when overheated by panting with its mouth open; when too cold, it retracts its extremities and

Food and Water

appears sluggish.

It is useless to warm turtles at feeding time and then allow temperatures to drop again. Under such conditions the ingested food cannot be digested but simply decomposes in the stomach. If for some reason turtles must be kept at lower temperatures for a brief period of time, do not feed them at all.

A well-fed and properly housed pet turtle can go several weeks without food if necessary. During vacation it is advisable to feed the animal heavily for several days prior to departure. Then simply leave it in a clean, heated tank, unfed, until you return; feed heavily upon your return.

Calcium

All turtles, and especially hatchlings, require large amounts of calcium and phosphorus with which to build their shells. Several calcium and/or calcium-vitamin preparations for turtles are available, and all are easily added to the food. It is best to use powdered combinations, as these may be sprinkled lightly over vegetable material or thoroughly mixed with meat before feeding.

Tortoises and larger aquatic turtles may be fed powdered oyster shell by mixing it with their food. This is often sold in feed stores for use with chickens. Tortoises will usually eat this material readily from a small, low dish. In lieu of this, or in the case of small hatchlings, a hardened block of plaster of Paris may be placed in the cage or in the aquarium water. Most petshops sell these under various trade names.

How often

Hatchlings, small turtles, and tortoises should be fed once daily, several hours after the basking light has been turned on and the temperatures are at an optimum. Large turtles, 5 inches and over, need be fed only three or four times per week. In either case, the turtle should be fed all it will readily consume in ten to 15 minutes.

Important: Remember, because an aquatic turtle's tongue is fixed in place, he *cannot* swallow food unless the water is deep enough for him to submerge his head.

Food and Water

Aquatics

All food should be cut or chopped to a size that can be swallowed readily. This includes plant material, but lettuce leaves can be placed in the water to be browsed upon. The diet should be three-fourths meat and one-fourth vegetable material. **Feed:** Scraped or diced beef, chopped fish, chopped small *whole* fish such as minnows, canned dog food, chopped beef or chicken liver, beef heart, beef kidneys, earthworms. Hatchlings enjoy tubifex worms, whiteworms, glassworm larvae and mosquito larvae, as well as adult brine shrimp. Some species readily take chopped raw shrimp in the shell. **Do not** feed hamburger. Feed also small pieces of tomato, mashed berries of any kind, green lettuce such as romaine, shredded spinach, and bunched aquarium plants such as elodea. The latter has the advantage of remaining attractive in the tank until it is eaten, and it is inexpensive.

Terrestrial

Tortoises require more food in

Most turtles, aquatic or terrestrial, will eat at least occasional meals containing such items as mushrooms, lettuce, and berries.

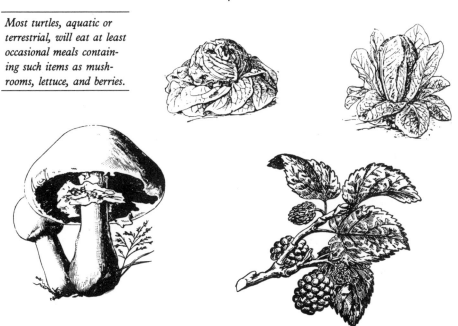

15

Food and Water

relation to their size than do the aquatic species. They also need considerable fiber, which is usually supplied by feeding lettuce. A 4-inch tortoise should consume 1 to 1½ cups of food per day. Always feed in the same spot and, if possible, at the same time every day. Do not remove uneaten food too soon, for tortoises do a good deal of browsing. Be certain that all fruits and vegetables are thoroughly washed before feeding.

Water should not be left standing in a tortoise tank; remove the animals to a shallow basin and allow them to drink their fill. The diet should consist of 80% plant matter and 20% meat.

Feed: *Green* lettuce, such as romaine (large amounts), tender cabbage leaves, spinach, cooked sweet potatoes, raw squash coarsely grated, cucumber, carrot, corn on the cob, and fruits of all kinds, especially berries, melons, peaches, apples, and tomatoes. Meat should be provided in the form of canned dog food.

Those products that are red in color will be more readily taken than others. Incidentally, if a tortoise is slow to feed, try mashed banana colored red with food coloring; with some desert species yellow is the preferred color. Small amounts of high quality leafy hay such as alfalfa are relished by many tortoises and make an excellent browsing food.

Captions for color pages 17 through 24
Kinixys belliana, *a South African tortoise; photo by Dr. Herbert R. Axelrod; p. 17 top. The painted turtle* Chrysemys picta picta; *photo by Dr. Herbert R. Axelrod; p. 17 bottom. A hatchling slider,* Pseudemys concinna hieroglyphica; *photo by Dr. Herbert R. Axelrod; p. 18 top.* Chelodina longicollis, *an Australian longneck; photo by Dr. Herbert R. Axelrod; p. 18 bottom.* Mauremys caspica, *the Caspian turtle; photo by Dr. Herbert R. Axelrod; p. 19 top.* Chrysemys picta picta, *a painted turtle; photo by Dr. Herbert R. Axelrod; p. 19 bottom. Two views of a hatchling slider,* Pseudemys concinna hieroglyphica; *photos by Dr. Herbert R. Axelrod; p. 20. The red-eared turtle,* Pseudemys scripta elegans; *photo by Dr. Herbert R. Axelrod; p. 21 top.* Emydoidea blandingi, *Blanding's box turtle; photo by Dr. Herbert R. Axelrod; p. 21 bottom.* Mauremys leprosa, *the Spanish turtle; photo by G. Marcuse; p. 22 top. A young* Podocnemis erythrocephala; *photo by Dr. Herbert R. Axelrod; p. 22 bottom. Red-legged tortoises,* Geochelone carbonaria; *photo by Harald Schultz; p. 23 top. The matamata,* Chelus fimbriatus; *photo by Harald Schultz; p. 23 bottom.* Chinemys reevesi; *photo by Dr. Herbert R. Axelrod; p. 24 top.* Geochelone gigantea, *the Aldabra tortoise; photo by Dr. Herbert R. Axelrod; p. 24 bottom.*

17

Turtle Care

Any captive animal survives and prospers in direct ratio to the type of care it receives. Turtles do not have many requirements, but those that they do have are *absolutely necessary* to their well-being. Note again that these are living creatures, and by keeping them the owner incurs an obligation. Note also that no one can lay down hard and fast rules about animal care and guarantee success. Animals, even turtles, are individuals, and the successful keeper varies basic procedures to suit the specimen in hand.

HOUSING

Aquatics

For sliders, cooters, painted turtles, snappers, soft-shells, side-necks, map turtles, and similar species, provide as large an aquarium or tank as possible. If the container is to be kept in an air-conditioned room, it should be high enough to permit use of a cover glass. Remember, however, that the container will have to be cleaned frequently and therefore should be relatively easy to handle. Larger size aquariums may be filtered using standard filters sold for use with tropical fish. Outside box filters are more efficient for use with turtles and easier to modify for use with shallow water (extend the siphon and return tubes). Undergravel filters are not suitable.

A 2½-gallon standard size aquarium is adequate for two or three hatchling sliders or one small soft-shell. A larger tank, say 10 or 15 gallons, can be decorated with ornamental rocks and plants (either natural or artificial) and will present a more pleasing addition to the home. In lieu of an aquarium, many household plastic containers can be substituted, provided they are large enough (2 to 3 gallons) and can be covered.

The "turtle bowls" commonly sold to house hatchling pet turtles are too shallow, cannot be covered, do not provide adequate basking area, are too small, and cannot be heated. Use them only if no other container is available.

The container floor should be covered with regular well-washed aquarium gravel to a depth of ½ to 1 inch. Soft-shells will require 2 inches of gravel, at least. The container should be filled with at least 2 inches of tepid water. If the size of the container permits, 4 to 6

Turtle Care

In most of the southeastern states of the U.S. various species of sliders or cooters, genus Pseudemys, are abundant. They are found in almost all larger bodies of water, from ponds to lakes and rivers. Although they are readily recognized as sliders, their specific identification is often very difficult.

inches is even better for the turtles and presents a more pleasing picture. With soft-shells, the water line should be determined by the turtle: soft-shells should be able to reach the surface simply by stetching their necks upward; usually a water depth of one and one-half to two times the length of carapace is correct.

Now provide a basking spot. This may be of any material that is not abrasive. It is well to avoid bricks, rough stones, concrete, etc. The finest possible material for a basking site is natural cork bark, which usually can be obtained from florists or window dressers. It may be cut to size and jammed across one end of the tank, allowing one edge to dip into the water. Be careful that it fits the tank snugly or a specimen may become lodged in a crevice and injure itself or drown. Alternatively, the bark can simply be floated on the surface, provided the edges allow the turtles to climb on easily. Whatever is used, remember that it should not be abrasive, yet should allow some grip for the turtle's claws. It should provide easy access and be easily cleanable.

Further decorations may be added if desired, such as plastic plants, a piece of log, etc. Avoid unsoaked wood, however, as it may contain substances harmful to the turtles.

Slider hatchlings are frequently kept in aquaria with fishes. This is fine, provided the water is low enough to prevent the turtle climbing out and provided a "raft" is furnished on which the turtle can bask.

In addition to what you feed him, a turtle in an aquarium will eat small snails and may chew some of the plants. While there are reports of turtles molesting the fish, this appears to be fairly rare. Most turtles will, however, eat dead fishes.

Bog or marsh types

For box turtles, wood turtles, spotted turtles, and similar species the housing is merely a modification of the aquatic setup. A larger land area should be provided, while the water area is considerably shallower. Requirements vary between hatchlings and adult specimens, however.

Box turtles are the most terrestrial of this group. All of the box turtles other than the ornate box may be housed in a tank that is first floored with aquarium sand and half the area then covered with flat stones or cork bark. One-half to 1 inch of water is

Turtle Care

added, forming a shallow pool at the end of the tank opposite the stones. The ornate box turtle may be housed in this same setup, with the exception of the water. The animal should be removed thrice weekly and allowed to soak in shallow water in a sink or basin.

Similar tank arrangements satisfy the requirements of other large species, although water depth should be increased somewhat for larger specimens. Spotted turtles, especially, require water several inches deep. A 15-gallon tank of standard dimensions (24" × 12" × 12") will comfortably house two adult box turtles, one medium size wood turtle, or three adult spotted turtles.

Hatchling box and wood turtles should be housed in a tank layered with damp moss. These hatchlings are clumsy in water and often drown. It is best to remove and bathe them in shallow water in a basin where they can be supervised rather than to leave standing water in the tank.

Mention should be made here of the "terraria" advocated by many authors. Such units with several layers of stone, gravel, and soil are excellent for plants, but with turtles are of little value unless intensively cared for. The "duplication of nature" idea is what inspires such setups. Unfortunately, it is difficult to maintain this even in units of several square feet, and more so in small aquarium tanks. Small terraria become messy in a short time, plants are rapidly trampled, and the unit soon becomes an eyesore. Plastic plants that can be removed and washed provide a nice touch if they are firmly wedged in place with a few small rocks.

Terrestrials

European tortoises and gopher tortoises, among others, have the simplest cage requirements but are the most difficult to keep. Tortoises need ample room. A pair of 4- to 5-inch European tortoises requires at least a "long" 20-gallon tank (30" × 12" × 12"). Floor the tank with several inches of dry aquarium gravel or pebbles. A few flat stones and perhaps a plastic plant or two will fill the need for any decoration felt necessary.

An alternate method of equipping a tortoise tank is to floor the unit with several inches of dried, chopped sugar cane, widely sold as a litter for chickens. This is perhaps the best flooring medium for tortoises, as it allows them to burrow

28

and absorbs moisture quickly. Under no circumstances should fuller's earth, sold commercially under various trade names for use in cat boxes, be used. These clay products are dusty and can cause nasal and respiratory problems in tortoises. If swallowed, they can cause intestinal blockages. Also avoid the use of sawdust or cedar shavings.

Under no circumstances should standing water be left in a tank containing tortoises. Although the animals require water, they cannot survive extreme dampness or humidity for long. Tortoises should be watered by putting them in a separate basin of water three times weekly and allowing them to drink their fill. It should be mentioned that a turtle that has just drunk water should not be lifted in such a manner as to point the head downward. This may cause water to flow from the stomach into the lungs, with serious effects.

LIGHT AND HEAT

Captive chelonians cannot be expected to survive or remain in good health without light and heat. Both are *absolutely* essential to their well-being. Most aquatic turtles, especially hatchlings, should have some direct natural sunlight; sunlight shining through window glass is of no value to them. However, if you put turtles outdoors in small containers, watch them carefully or provide them with some shade. Sunlight can rapidly heat a small container to lethal temperatures.

Aquatics

Keep the tank water between 75 and 85°F. A small aquarium heater, with thermostat, can be kept in a jar of water and placed in the shallower water of the tank itself. Be certain the turtles cannot move the unit or claw the insulation loose.

In the absence of sunlight, provide an electric light to bask under. A "gooseneck" desk lamp, an aquarium reflector, or something similar is excellent. Place the bulb over the basking spot, allowing it to burn ten to 12 hours daily. Only incandescent lamps should be used for this purpose as fluorescent lamps do not give off either proper light or heat.

Turtles should not live in 80°F water and breathe 65°F air. If the room is air-conditioned, partially cover the tank with a loose-fitting piece of glass. A thermometer will quickly indicate how much coverage is needed. Caution is needed here, however, for covered tanks with a heater in the water and a basking lamp turned on will heat up quickly. Temperatures over 90°F are best avoided.

Bog and marsh types

These species have much the same light and heat requirements as the aquatics. In tanks housing them, a small flexible heat cable buried in the sand is preferable to other heating devices. Such a cable distributes the required heat evenly over the floor of the tank. A basking lamp is required.

Terrestrials

Tortoises *must* have heat in the

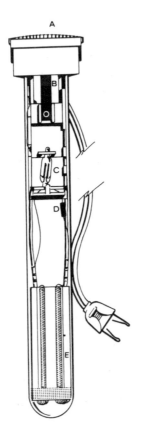

Ordinary aquarium heaters that can be purchased in any petshop are satisfactory for use with aquatic turtles if the water level is kept high enough to cover the tube of the heater. You may have to cover the glass tube with hardware cloth to prevent large, active turtles from breaking it, however.

Parts of an aquarium heater-thermostat combination.

(A) Temperature adjustment.

(B) Bi-metal thermostat.

(C) Pilot light.

(D) Condenser (to eliminate static).

(E) Heating coil.

flooring materials. A small heating cable is most practical and can be equipped with a thermostat. It is wise to cover such a cable with a thin piece of masonite prior to flooring the tank. This will prevent the tortoises from digging up the cable and damaging either it or themselves.

Failing this, the tank may be raised upon a wooden base with a light bulb placed under one end only. With such an arrangement a 40-W bulb enclosed beneath one end of the tank will keep a 20-gallon tank sufficiently warm. If the area above the bulb becomes too warm, the tortoises can move to the unheated, cooler area. This "ground heat" can be turned off at night. Under no circumstances should a tortoise tank be completely covered, as this promotes a degree of humidity that is often fatal.

Tortoises should be provided with a light for basking like that provided for aquatics.

Hibernation

As we mentioned, the physiology of cold-blooded animals does not allow them to regulate their body temperatures internally. In those climates where there is a cold winter, such animals must enter a state of what is essentially suspended animation. As their temperatures

The three U.S. species of true tortoises belonging to the genus Gopherus *are found only in the warmest areas of the country. They are all called gopher tortoises because the eastern* G. polyphemus *hibernates in gopher holes during the mild Florida winter.*

Turtle Care

fall with the falling thermometer, they can no longer function normally; they cannot avoid enemies, feed, or drink. They gradually become sluggish and spend more and more time hidden away in burrows or buried in mud. Oxygen intake is reduced to the barest minimum and the heart beat slows.

The metabolic rate is greatly reduced, and the animal is able to survive by using its surplus fat as an energy source. As spring approaches, temperatures gradually rise, and with them the animal's metabolism. At the proper time, the animal emerges from its deep sleep to resume its normal life. Hibernation is an *extremely gradual* process at both its onset and eventual emergence. Hibernation quarters are always somewhat below the usual freezing point, but it often happens that a severe frost lowers the temperature too far below, and many hibernating animals die.

Hibernation in captivity

Some authors suggest that captive turtles be allowed or even encouraged to hibernate, but to hibernate a captive turtle or tortoise properly the specimen must be in extremely good physical condition, with a noticeable excess of fat. It must be provided with a large box of slightly dampened leaves, hay, or similar material and allowed to burrow in and out at will. When the animal begins to stay buried for several days at a time, the container should be moved into an area where the temperature will remain a relatively constant 40 to 50°F until the following spring. Some water should be added from time to time to keep the hibernating material slightly damp—a difficult thing to judge. When temperatures begin to rise in the spring and all danger of frost is past, the box is placed outdoors and the animal allowed to gradually awaken. Disturbing a specimen while it is in forced hibernation usually results in its death, so captive animals should either hibernate or be kept at optimum temperatures; hatchlings of any species should **not** be hibernated at all.

Personally, I prefer to see captive animals maintained at optimum temperatures the year around, because in my experience the survival rate of captive hibernating animals is relatively low. Also, it is unnecessary, since captive animals do not require a winter sleep to remain in good health.

Turtles Outdoors

If space such as a back yard or patio is available, pet turtles will benefit greatly by spending the summer months outdoors. If adult turtles are kept, outdoor enclosures are about the only practical way an amateur collector can keep them.

Several types of containers lend themselves to temporary outdoor cages. Many large pet shops and garden shops sell inexpensive plastic or fiberglass "lily" pools. These may be buried in the ground or left free-standing and are especially good for hatchlings. Stock watering tanks are available in many shapes and sizes and usually include a drain plug. Such tanks should be raised on bricks or concrete blocks in a manner that puts the tank on a slight slant toward the drain. If desired, the exterior may be masked with a rock garden. The interior should be arranged like an indoor aquarium. However, remember to place the basking spots in the *center* of the pools. If left near the side, the turtles may be able to climb over and escape.

All outside turtle tanks should be covered, especially if they house hatchlings or small specimens, to protect the turtles from being killed or injured by predatory birds, wandering cats, and curious children. Covers are easily constructed of hardware cloth tacked to a wooden frame. Do not use plastic or pliofilm as a cover. These will cause the pool to overheat, possibly to a lethal temperature under bright sunlight. Arrange it so that part of the pool is always shaded. This way, your pets can select the temperature they prefer.

Metal stock tanks should be wiped thoroughly with vinegar, then rinsed and allowed to dry. The application of several coats of rubberized swimming pool paint will enhance the interior appearance

Because of current restrictions on the sale of small turtles, you may be forced to collect your own, Never collect more than you need and always check local laws before collecting.

Ailments

and will prevent the turtles' being poisoned by any soluble chemical which might be present in the galvanizing.

Permanent outdoor enclosures are easily built of bricks or concrete blocks. The walls surrounding the area should be about 30 inches high and provided with an overhang at the top, especially at the corners, as many species are amazing climbers. A pool is easily constructed of smooth concrete, preferably with a drain for cleaning purposes. Such pools should be about 1 foot in depth and have gently sloping sides, allowing even clumsy species like the box turtle to enter and leave easily. Permanent enclosures, like smaller tanks, are best covered. Be certain to provide plenty of hiding spots and shady areas.

A carefully selected specimen, kept under proper conditions, will seldom be subject to illness. Assuming the specimen is healthy to begin with, any illness it later contracts will almost invariably be the fault of poor feeding, improper housing, or both.

Inasmuch as there is no way of knowing how well turtles were cared for prior to sale, it is advisable that the owner of a new turtle treat it prophylactically as soon as possible. The most effective way of doing this is to isolate the newly purchased turtle in a small glass or plastic tank. The water used in this tank should be a solution of a water-soluble antibiotic, such as oxytetracycline hydrochloride. This is usually sold in 250 mg capsules. Open the capsule and dissolve the contents in a few ounces of warm water. This is sufficient to treat ten gallons of tank water. For smaller quantities, divide the *powder* proportionately. The solution is stable for only 12 to 24 hours. This broad spectrum antibiotic can usually be purchased at feed stores, as it is widely used for treating chickens, calves, and lambs. Many petshops sell antibiotic tablets for use with birds. These may be used with turtles. In the United Kingdom and some other areas a veterinarian's or doctor's

Ailments

prescription is required to purchase antibiotics. Regardless of which is used, it should be dissolved in water according to instructions given for use with birds. Sufficient solution should be mixed to attain a water depth deep enough for the turtle to swim. Keep the turtle in this solution for five days, after which it can be placed in its permanent home. The solution should be changed completely each day of the five-day treatment.

Prophylactic treatment for new arrivals is particularly important if there are other turtles in the collection. This treatment is especially effective in curbing respiratory diseases and difficult-to-diagnose gastric ailments.

Soft shell

This, probably the most common ailment of hatchlings and young turtles, is the result of feeding a diet deficient in calcium and other essential vitamins and minerals. If not too far advanced, the condition can be reversed by increasing the amount of calcium and vitamins in the diet. If a calcium additive such as bone meal or tricalcium carbonate (packaged for dogs) is not available at the local petshop, calcium carbonate is available as a fine powder from any druggist. Liberal quantities of this chemical should be added to the food. Be certain also that the animals receive some multivitamin and mineral powder daily. For complete recovery, three elements are essential: calcium and phosphorus in approximately a 5:1 proportion, plus vitamin D. The latter the turtle's back can manufacture by itself, but only in the presence of sunlight. For this reason, specimens with soft shell should be given every opportunity to bask in full sunlight. The recovery from soft shell is a long and tedious process, and improvement takes several weeks or longer.

Swollen eyes

This, another common ailment, especially of hatchlings, is also usually caused by improper diet and incorrect housing. Swollen eyes are often initiated, and always aggravated, by dirty water. Check the chapters on care and feeding and make such corrections in diet and housing as may be indicated. Increase the wattage of the basking light and allow the turtle to bask in direct sunlight, if possible. Antibiotic eye ointments are useful

Ailments

but must be applied to the *inside* of the eyelids to be effective. The broad end of a flat toothpick can be used to part the swollen lids during application. When using ointments, avoid smearing them over the animal's nostrils.

Fungus

This appears as grayish or whitish patches on the turtle's skin. It does not attack the shell. Fungus usually develops only on turtles that cannot

Diamondback terrapins, Malaclemys, *are found in brackish to salt water. If some salt is not added to their water they tend to rapidly develop fungus infections. Because they are edible and are fished commercially, these turtles are among the few that have open and closed seasons during which they may or may not be taken.*

dry off completely when basking. It will also attack brackish water species (diamondback terrapins) when they are kept in fresh water.

Fungus is easily treated. Purchase a tropical fish "ich" remedy containing malachite green. Add three or four drops of this to a dish of water and leave the turtle in this solution for five minutes twice a day. Make a fresh solution each time. Note that fish fungus is sometimes treated with potassium permanganate; this should definitely be avoided. To prevent recurrences, one heaping teaspoonful of non-iodized salt should be added to each gallon of aquarium water. Rearrange or enlarge the basking area to permit

Ailments

thorough drying. If possible, expose the turtle to strong sunlight. Maintain the salt solution for several weeks.

Shell rot

This usually appears in the form of sores or gray spots on the plastron (undershell). It is usually caused by basking areas that are abrasive or sand that is too sharp. Correct the physical conditions, replacing rough stones with water-worn wood or cork bark.

Such injuries usually heal themselves if the cause is removed. If the spots are raw or bleeding, treat them twice daily with an antibiotic ointment containing neomycin, available at petshops or drug stores. The turtle should be kept dry for an hour after treatment.

Red leg

This is an ailment usually seen in amphibians, particularly frogs. However, it occurs in captive soft-shell turtles. Red leg is caused by a breakdown of the surface capillaries, and a soft-shell turtle suffering from the disease will show a red flush over the legs and plastron. Treatment consists of keeping the animal in an oxytetracycline solution.

Worms

These are seldom seen in hatchlings, although many varieties do infest turtles, especially adults. If they are present in the droppings, proper cage sanitation will eventually eliminate them by preventing the eggs from being reingested. In persistent cases, intestinal worms may usually be eliminated with piperazine, a vermifuge available from veterinarians, who can also advise on the dosage. Parasites are seldom a cause for concern to the owner of a few pet turtles.

Pneumonia

This name is usually given to a respiratory ailment characterized by a general sluggishness, closed eyes, labored and wheezing breath, and a bubbling nose. It is especially common in tortoises. Again, improper cage conditions and diet create the conditions allowing disease to infect the specimens. A well-fed specimen can usually withstand an occasional sudden chill

Ailments

or a brief period of dampness, but quarters that are consistently below proper temperatures, or in the case of tortoises too damp, almost always result in the animal's having respiratory problems. The antibiotic used as initial prophylaxis, oxytetracycline hydrochloride (Terramycin), is effective. Cage conditions should be improved and every effort should be made to induce the invalid to eat.

In addition to frequently being fatal, respiratory diseases are usually highly contagious to cage mates. Once the illness does appear, the affected turtle should be isolated and all cage mates put through the prophylactic treatment. In the case of tortoises, the dry powder should be sprinkled on the food in addition to being placed in the drinking water. Use a bulb or other convenient source of heat to maintain a constant temperature between 80 and 85°F. This must be done around the clock, until all symptoms have gone.

If a specimen has difficulty in breathing, place it in a small closed plastic box containing a dish holding a wad of cotton soaked with hot water and few drops of oil of eucalyptus. The dish containing the cotton should be immovable, and the box should not be so airtight that it suffocates the turtle. The object is to create a warm, steamy atmosphere for several hours.

When pneumonia is suspected, it is advisable, especially in the case of valuable specimens, to consult a veterinarian.

Off feed

This is not a disease, but nevertheless it is a common complaint of turtle owners. Almost invariably a turtle or tortoise that consistently refuses to eat is being kept improperly. Check all cage conditions, especially temperature, and offer a change in diet. A reticent box turtle will often feed voraciously when presented with a few blackberries instead of the usual canned dog food. Excessive or abusive handling, usually by children, does a turtle no good and often prevents its feeding. Again, one should remember that pet turtles are not toys.

Salmonellosis

This is an intestinal ailment of turtles caused by an organism called *Salmonella*. Use of the prophylactic treatment recommended for newly

Ailments

acquired specimens will usually prevent its appearance in pet turtles. The disease is not easily recognized by the layman: accurate diagnosis involves both microscopical and bacterial culture work. When suffering from the disease, tortoises sometimes have a loose, greenish stool, often blood-streaked.

Salmonellosis is mentioned here primarily because hatchling native turtles were found to be passive vectors of certain strains of salmonella several years ago. The knowledge that a turtle could act as carrier of a disease affecting humans caused thousands of pet turtles to be needlessly destroyed. I say needlessly because the chances of a person's contracting salmonella from an animal are extremely remote, and this is especially so of pet turtles kept under proper conditions. Salmonella bacteria (there are several hundred species) are found very widely in nature. Not only dogs, cats, birds and poultry, but humans also can be, and often are, passive vectors of salmonella, as well as of many other bacteria. Cleanliness and antibiotics are the best precautions.

The salmonellosis scare, however, led to the passage of many local and state laws regarding the sale of turtles, some of which are still in effect. Thus in many areas hatchling water turtles can no longer be sold, and in some cases there are even laws prohibiting the sale of any turtles or tortoises under 3, 4, or even 5 inches in shell length.

Mites (such as these chiggers) are often found on wild-collected turtles and may occasionally spread to the keeper. They are easily controlled by several insecticide powders and strips. Use caution whenever any insecticide is used near reptiles, including turtles, as they are very sensitive to most anti-insect products.

Sexing and Breeding

Usually, but not always, the males of aquatic species have long, tapering tails that are thick at the base. Males of many species, for example *Pseudemys* and *Chrysemys* species, have the nails of the front feet greatly elongated. Almost invariably, males are smaller than females, but this characteristic is of little value in determining sex. When the tail is extended, the cloacal opening of the male is beyond the margin of the carapace.

Females of the aquatic species have short stubby tails, short blunt nails on the front feet, and are usually distinctly larger than males.

Their cloacal opening does not reach beyond the carapace.

Male box turtles often have red eyes and brighter colors on the forelegs than do the females. Female box turtles frequently have brown eyes and a somewhat broader shell.

Sexing turtles is usually easy, as many species have sexually different adult sizes, shell shapes, and color patterns. Box turtles, however, are most readily sexed by the presence of a distinct concavity or depression in the posterior part of the male's plastron that is absent in the female's.

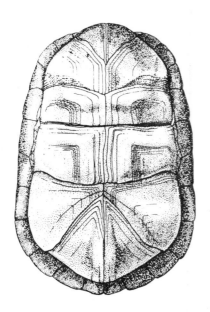
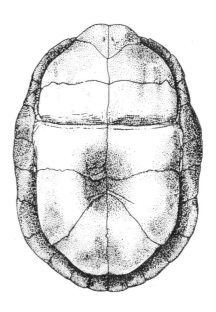

Sexing and Breeding

Hatchling turtles are often very different in general appearance from the adults. Commonly the shell is brightly colored, may have distinct patterns absent in adults, and may even be a different shape. The umbilical scar is visible in many hatchlings and may remain as a distinct round or elongated area of exposed tissue for several months. The umbilical area is especially prone to fungus attacks and should be checked regularly.

Sexing and Breeding

Male tortoises (and some aquatic species) have a deeply concave plastron and often a projecting spur at the front edge immediately beneath the chin. They also have longer tails than the females, sometimes with a prominent, curved spur at the tip. These sexual characteristics apply to the tortoises mentioned in this book. While many other tortoises share these characteristics, they should not be

MALE

The various species of sliders (Pseudemys) are probably best sexed by a combination of adult size (females often much larger than males), coloration (males often very dark both on the skin and the shell), and front claws and tail length (longer in the male). Occasionally males also have a distinctly concave plastron like that of male box turtles.

FEMALE

used to judge species other than those mentioned.

Turtles will breed in captivity, but the requirements are usually beyond the facilities of the amateur. Courtship is varied, often elaborate, and is usually possible only in commodious quarters.

Hatching eggs

In the event that a captive pet turtle should produce a batch of eggs or a collector acquire turtle eggs laid in the wild, they may be hatched by this method.

The upper surface of each egg should be marked with pencil so that this mark can always be kept uppermost during incubation, for reptile embryos are usually killed if the egg is turned. The eggs are placed on a layer of damp paper towelling or sterilized peat moss on the bottom of a bowl or plastic bag. They should then be surrounded and lightly covered with more damp towelling or moistened peat moss. Use one material or the other, not both. The bowl should then be loosely covered with a piece of glass, or if a bag is used the mouth should be tied shut. Unless mold appears, nothing further need be done.

Proper moisture content can be gauged by the droplets of

Sexing and Breeding

condensation that form on the inside of the glass or plastic. If they do not appear, the hatching medium should be lightly sprinkled. If mold appears, the eggs should be carefully removed and wiped clean with a damp cloth, carefully holding each egg upright. Fresh towelling or peat moss should be used and the eggs replaced in their original position.

Keep the container in a quiet, preferably dark place where a reasonably constant temperature of between 80 and 90°F can be maintained. Depending on the temperature, the eggs should hatch

At hatching baby turtles have a small egg tooth on the snout that is used to cut open the leathery egg shell. This is lost in a few hours to a few days.

in from five to ten weeks. When hatching begins, do not disturb the young or attempt to assist them in any way. The young turtles upon hatching often spend several days in the shell while they are absorbing the remnants of the yolk; disturbance during this period can result in rupturing of the blood vessels, which may be fatal.

Exotic Turtles

Petshops in the larger cities and specialist reptile dealers often have unusual species of exotic turtles and tortoises for sale. Although most can be cared for in the manner already outlined, many have highly specialized requirements. Accurate identification is necessary in order to provide proper care. Often, local zoos or museums can advise you on this, or you can consult the literature usually available in large libraries. If an exotic species is purchased, it is well to remember that a specimen living under a given set of conditions in the dealer's shop will not necessarily *survive* under similar conditions in the home.

Among the exotic species that appear with some regularity in shops, the following are noteworthy because of their unusual characteristics. The matamata (*Chelus fimbriatus*) from South America, which closely resembles a piece of waterlogged wood, is equipped with many loose flaps of skin on the head and neck. These flaps assist the turtle in locating its primary food, which is live fishes. Matamatas require high temperatures but should not be exposed to bright lights. They will drown in water over several inches deep, as they are poor swimmers at best and breathe by stretching their necks to the surface. A matamata will take fresh-killed or even thawed-out frozen fish if it is cut into or is in the shape of an appropriately sized fish and is tossed into or waved about in the water so that it appears to be "swimming" in front of the turtle. Matamatas capture their prey by remaining motionless until it is right in front of them and then inhaling it suddenly.

The flap-shell turtle (*Lissemys punctata*), from India, is a member of the soft-shell group. The animal is equipped with a shell that is hinged in a manner that allows it to completely enclose its head, forequarters, hindquarters, and tail, with special flaps for each. It requires high temperatures, deep water, and fish or shrimp as food.

The pancake tortoise (*Malacochersus tornieri*) from East Africa is a terrestrial species in which the underlying bone plates of the shell are resorbed as the animal grows older. This results in the horny scutes being supported by a thin, netlike foundation of bone. Such a shell structure enables the animal to squeeze into narrow crevices where, like many lizards, it inflates its body until it is tightly wedged in its rocky retreat. Captives must have a narrow, flat box to squeeze under. They require high

Exotic Turtles

temperatures and a wide variety of fresh fruits and vegetables.

Species such as those listed above are usually expensive, often in the $50-$100 range. Such an investment again underscores the need for proper care and housing so often mentioned in this book. The purchase of many foreign species now requires special permits and paperwork; a reputable dealer will be able to guide you through this important but often frustrating step in turtle ownership.

Many species of turtles occasionally show up at specialty dealers, but these are often very expensive and may have quite a bit of paperwork required because of conservation laws. This is the unusually colorful Indian peacock soft-shell, Trionyx hurum.

Conservation

Exploding human population, air and water pollution, habitat destruction, and uncontrolled use of insecticides all present problems for mankind and reflect his overall disregard for the natural world he lives in and on. Such conditions also destroy man's fellow creatures. Today, everyone is aware that hundreds of species are already in immediate danger of becoming extinct because of them.

For the most part, turtles are not exempt from this danger. Certain species, such as the red-eared slider, are bred and hatched under controlled conditions. These species are in no great present danger. However, gross exploitation of hatchlings of wild-breeding species such as the orange-spotted sideneck while at the same time adults are being collected wholesale for food and the onslaught of civilization is destroying their habitat can soon reduce the population to a point from which it cannot recover. Certainly there is nothing wrong with keeping pet turtles. However, keeping rare species just because they are rare, or even fairly common species under conditions in which they cannot survive, cannot in any way be justified. Properly kept, the common forms are just as interesting, just as colorful, and certainly hardier in captivity than are the rarities.

Most people keep pet animals in their homes because they wish to have a piece of nature close to them. Happily this is still possible; but over-exploitation of any species—whether turtles, leopards, monkeys, or ocelots—will soon result in a barren world. Think about it!

Turtles Considered Endangered or Threatened

Batagur baska—S.E. Asia
Clemmys muhlenbergi—U.S.
Geochelone elephantopus—Galapagos
Geochelone radiata—Madagascar
Geochelone yniphora—Madagascar
Morenia ocellata—Burma
Podocnemis expansa—South America
Podocnemis unifilis—South America
Psammobates geometrica—South Africa
Pseudemydura umbrina—Australia
Terrapene coahuila—Mexico
Trionyx ater—Mexico

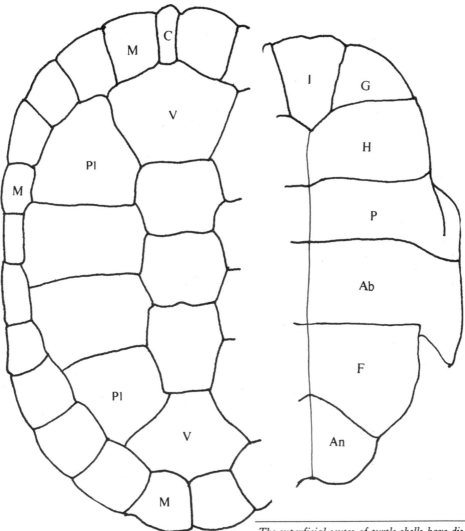

The superficial scutes of turtle shells have distinct names depending on their position. The upper shell, the carapace, is shown to the left, with the lower shell, the plastron, to the right. Carapace: *C = cervical; V = vertebrals; Pl = costals or pleurals; M = marginals.* Plastron: *I = intergular; G = gular; H = humeral; P = pectoral; Ab = abdominal; F = femoral; An = anal. Only half of the paired scutes are shown.*

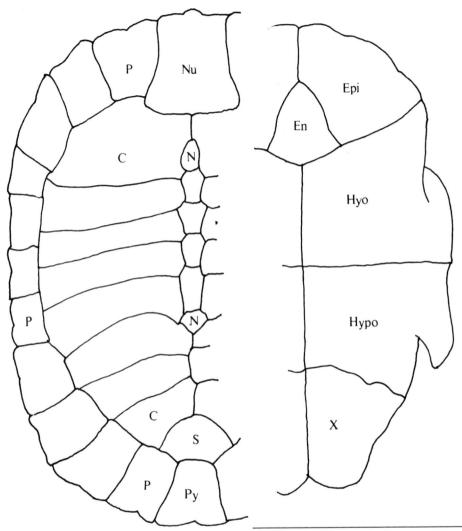

The bones of the turtle shell are very different from the visible horny scutes. The carapace is shown on the left, the plastron on the right, with only half of the paired bones shown. Carapace: *Nu = nuchal; N = neurals; P = peripherals; C = costals; S = suprapygal; Py = pygal.* Plastron: *En = entoplastron; Epi = epiplastron; Hyo = hyoplastron; Hypo = hypoplastron; X = xiphiplastron.*

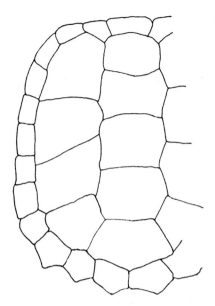

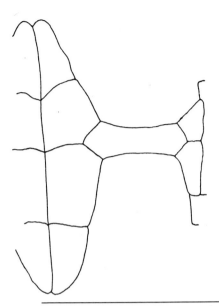

Carapace and plastron of the snapping turtle, Chelydra serpentina.

Carapace and plastron of a mud turtle, Kinosternon *species.*

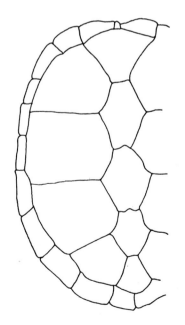

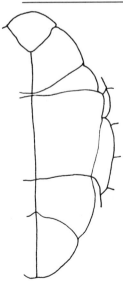

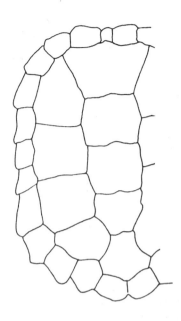

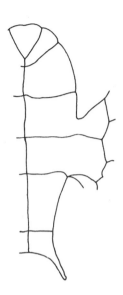

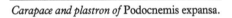

Carapace and plastron of Chelus fimbriatus, *the matamata.*

Carapace and plastron of Podocnemis expansa.

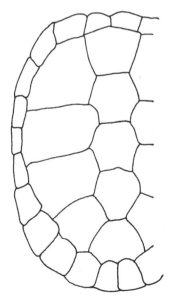

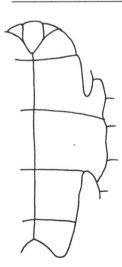

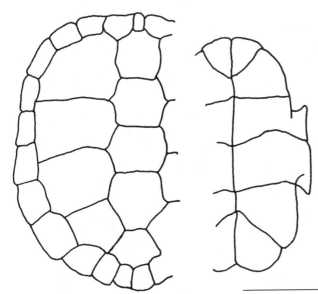

Carapace and plastron of a slider, Pseudemys
species.

Carapace and plastron of a tortoise, Geochelone *species.*

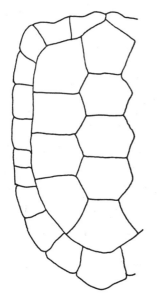

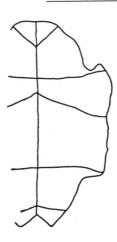

Identification

In keeping any animal, it is always preferable to prepare the home first, then get the specimen.

Unfortunately, the situation is often reversed, and the new pet owner finds himself keeping the turtle in pots, old dishes, or the bathtub. We will assume that the prospective turtle fancier reading this book would strike the "happy medium" and purchase specimens and container at the same time.

However, there are several dozen different species of turtles sold at one time or another, and many require different environments. Additional species are available from time to time from specialist reptile dealers, but these are beyond the scope of the beginner. If you should obtain one of these oddities, best check its requirements carefully. In order to know what type of environment is needed, we must first know what species we have. The key to identification will help us to do this.

Although in many turtles the scales of the head are more or less fused, in some they are quite distinct. The names of the head scales are: 1 = rostral; 2 = mental; 3 = nasals; 4 = upper labial; 5 = lower labial; 6 = postmandibular; 7 = frontonasal; 8 = prefrontals; 9 = frontal; 10 = supraoculars; 11 = frontoparietal; 12 = temporals; 13 = postoculars; 14 = parietals; 15 = interparietal; 16 = tympanum; 17 = supratympanum.

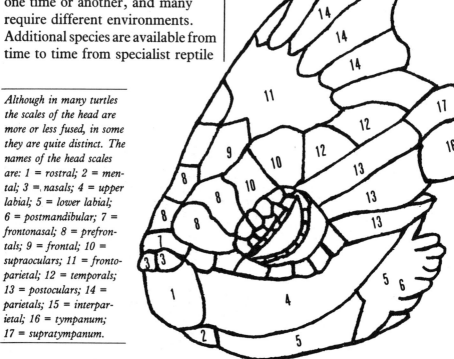

Identification

KEY TO COMMON NATIVE AND IMPORTED TURTLES IN THE UNITED STATES

To understand this key, we must first explain a few simple zoological terms for those of us who have forgotten our biology. Scientific names of animals are used for descriptive precision—they are the same all over the world. For example, there are well over three dozen species of turtles with the local name "green"; all are different in form and color shade, habitat (environment), and habits.

Obviously, then, to say "green turtle" is meaningless. However, when we say "*Chelonia mydas*" we are referring *specifically* and *only* to the green sea turtle. Many "scientific" names have been adapted into everyday language; for example, *Clemmys muhlenbergi* is known as "Muhlenberg's turtle" and *Chinemys reevesi* as "Reeves' turtle."

Clemmys muhlenbergi, *the bog or Muhlenberg's turtle, is currently on several state endangered species lists. It has never been commonly collected, partially because of its habitat in very shallow bog streams in the eastern U.S. Today its main threat is bulldozers draining its territory to make room for another condominium.*

Identification

It is also desirable to familiarize oneself with certain descriptive terms used in zoology, because they are clear, concise, universally understood (by turtle lovers as well as biologists), and they refer to specific areas of a turtle.

Mud turtles, genus Kinosternon, *are found over much of North and South America and are often common in ponds, lakes, and even ditches. There are several species in the United States, including the very common K.* subrubrum *found over much of the eastern half of the United States. They are often nuisances to fishermen, as they are great bait stealers. Although not colorful, they feed well in captivity (although their fishy diet may produce a foul odor) and make passable pets.*

Carapace	Upper shell
Plastron	Lower shell
Bridge	Joint between carapace and plastron
Scutes	Shields which cover the carapace and plastron
Vertebrals	Scutes down the center of the carapace
Costals	Scutes on either side of the vertebrals
Marginals	Scutes at the edge of the carapace
Ventral	Lower surface
Dorsal	Upper surface
Reticulations	Fine netlike or wavy markings

Identification

At one time hatchling red-eared sliders, Pseudemys scripta elegans, were the most commonly sold pet turtles, literally millions being bred in Louisiana each year for the pet trade. Thanks to the salmonellosis scare, however, this trade has been practically legislated out of existence. Subadults and adults are still occasionally available, however, and make good pets if you can afford the time to keep the water clean. Aquatic turtles are notoriously messy pets.

As an illustration of how *family, genus, species,* and *subspecies* are arranged, let us consider snapping turtles. They are turtle-like creatures, so they belong to the family Chelydridae. They also belong to the superfamily Cryptodira, which contains those turtles that retract their heads straight back into the shell, as distinguished from members of Pleurodira, which withdraw their necks by folding them sideways.

The snapping turtles are in the genus *Chelydra*. Each kind of snapping turtle has a species, or specific name, the most common being *serpentina*. There are several distinctive kinds of *Chelydra serpentina*, so each is given a subspecies name. For example, the Florida snapping turtle is known technically as *Chelydra serpentina osceola*. Incidentally, the name of the

Identification

genus is always capitalized and the species and subspecies names are always written in lower case, and all are italicized.

To use the key, study the specimen at hand carefully to determine the general color of the carapace. Specimens with the same or similar coloring are grouped together under the numerical "Carapace" headings. These main headings are subdivided into more specific descriptions of the various species. This key is not a precision tool; however, it should at least enable the turtle owner to find his specimen's place in a major group or genus. The reader should also remember that not all the species listed in the key will be available at any one time or place. In fact, some no longer enter the U.S. as they are on various local or federal endangered species list. All species listed in the key were at one time available, however, and most may be found in old, large collections.

DESCRIPTIVE KEY

1. **Carapace: Light or dark green;** flat and circular in shape; the head is retracted straight back into the shell.

A. Carapace has fine yellow or tan reticulations in each scute; ventral scutes have one or more open-centered black or brown blotches in each; head is striped with fine yellow lines; a prominent red blotch or stripe at the side of the head.

   Red-eared slider
   (*Pseudemys scripta*

Captions for color pages 57 through 64
A map turtle, Graptemys pseudogeographica; *photo by Dr. Herbert R. Axelrod; p. 57 top. A* Podocnemis expansa *laying her eggs; photo by Harald Schultz; p. 57 bottom. The Asian* Heosemys grandis; *photo by Mervin F. Roberts; p. 58 top. A colorful male box turtle,* Terrapene carolina; *photo by Dr. Herbert R. Axelrod; p. 58 bottom. A group of yellow-legged tortoises,* Geochelone denticulata, *captured for food; photo by Harald Schultz; p. 59 top.* Podocnemis expansa *captured for food; photo by Harald Schultz; p. 59 bottom. Two views of the South American sideneck* Phrynops geoffroanus; *photos by Dr. Herbert R. Axelrod; p. 60. Two views of* Podocnemis unifilis, *a sideneck once imported in numbers; photos by Dr. Herbert R. Axelrod; p. 61. The matamata,* Chelus fimbriatus; *photo by Dr. Herbert R. Axelrod; p. 62 top.* Podocnemis expansa; *photo by Harald Schultz; p. 62 bottom. Hatchlings of* Podocnemis unifilis *leaving the nest; photo by Harald Schultz; p. 63 top. A hatchling red-eared slider,* Pseudemys scripta elegans; *photo by Dr. Herbert R. Axelrod; p. 63 bottom. The yellow mud turtle,* Kinosternon flavescens; *photo by Dr. Herbert R. Axelrod; p. 64 top. The box turtle* Terrapene carolina bauri; *photo by Dr. Herbert R. Axelrod; p. 64 bottom.*

60

64

Identification

elegans), an aquatic species from the southern United States.

B. Carapace with yellow wavy reticulations in each scute; plastron tinged with orange; ventral markings absent or else confined to the seams between scutes; head is striped and blotched with yellow; a prominent yellow line on the chin; feet tinged with orange.

Slider (*Pseudemys concinna*), an aquatic species from the southern United States; five subspecies known.

C. Carapace slightly peaked; heavily marked with green and yellow, especially at outer edge of the rear marginals; plastron pale yellow; markings, if present, confined to the front edge; a large distinct yellow blotch on either side of the head.

Yellow-bellied turtle (*Pseudemys scripta scripta*), an aquatic from the southeastern United States; it sometimes interbreeds with the red-eared slider (*Pseudemys scripta elegans*).

D. Carapace has a black spot encircled by a yellow or pale green ring (ocellus) in each scute; plastron covered with a single large, netlike blotch; edges of the plastron ringed with orange or red; head finely striped with yellow; a red, yellow, or orange ear spot is present; three large yellow spots prominent on the chin.

Ornate slider (*Pseudemys scripta callirostris*), a cold-sensitive, tropical, aquatic species from northern South America.

2. **Carapace: Light tan or gray,** highly peaked with a central saw-toothed ridge; head retracted straight back into body.

A. Central ridge of the carapace with at least two definite spines; rear marginals serrated (toothed); plastron almost covered by a heavy, dark pattern; a definite yellow semi-circle behind the eye.

Mississippi map turtle (*Graptemys kohni*), a cold-sensitive aquatic species from the Mississippi Valley south of the Missouri.

65

B. Central ridge of the carapace distinctly serrated; spines are black; rear marginals heavily serrated; plastron almost covered by a heavy, dark pattern; head and neck striped with yellow, the stripes reaching the eye.

> **False map turtle** (*Graptemys pseudogeographica*), a cold-sensitive aquatic species from the south central United States.

3. **Carapace: Pale olive or gray,** smooth in appearance, no pattern. Vertebral scutes are quite broad; head drawn sidewise into the shell.

A. Head has a definite "nose"; several blotches of yellow, especially at temples and crown; plastron plain whitish-gray.

> **Yellow-spotted sideneck** (*Podocnemis unifilis*), a cold-sensitive tropical aquatic species from the Amazonian areas of South America; imports now restricted.

B. As for "A," except for blotches on the head, which are definite orange in color.

> **Orange-spotted sideneck** (*Podocnemis expansa*), a cold-sensitive tropical aquatic species from the Amazonian areas of South America; imports currently prohibited.

(**Note:** Although the foregoing sidenecks are hardy under proper captive conditions, rapidly reaching shell lengths of 8 to 10 inches, they are definitely shy animals and require special attention. Although *Podocnemis expansa* is legally protected in Brazil, large numbers of hatchlings are often "smuggled" out of that country and sold abroad illegally. This is unfortunate as many authorities consider this turtle to be faced with extinction.)

4. **Carapace: Black or very dark brown;** flat and circular in shape; head is retracted straight back into the shell.

A. Carapace quite flat; several varieties with tan bands across the carapace at the scute seams; marginals edged in bright red; plastron unmarked, pale yellow, or yellow suffused with red; a

Identification

Map turtles, genus Graptemys, are native to the southern U.S. and the Mississippi Valley, with over a dozen species and subspecies known. Some of these have very limited ranges in flowing, clean rivers, a habitat that is rapidly disappearing because of pollution and development. Although hatchlings of several Graptemys species once were sold with red-ears, map turtles are now specialty turtles, with most of the species commanding high prices (when they can be legally collected for sale). They seldom do well in captivity, however. Female map turtles may be two or three times larger than the males.

Identification

large black blotch may be present on the plastron; the neck, chin, and legs are striped with yellow and/or red.

Painted turtles (*Chrysemys picta*), aquatic turtles found over most of the eastern United States. Four subspecies are known: eastern painted turtle (*Chrysemys picta picta*), with an unmarked plastron; midland painted turtle (*Chrysemys picta marginata*), with a plastral marking confined to its center; western painted turtle (*Chrysemys picta belli*), with an intricate plastral pattern covering most of the ventral surface—adult western painted turtles are commonly sold as pets; southern painted turtle (*Chrysemys picta dorsalis*),

Painted turtles, Chrysemys picta, *are very much like small, flattened versions of sliders. In fact, many herpetologists (scientists who study reptiles and amphibians) feel that the slider genus* Pseudemys *should not be recognized and both the sliders and the painted turtle should be put into the single genus* Chrysemys. *Painted turtles are still common in much of their range and are often easily and legally collected. They make good pets. Many people collect a painted turtle locally in the spring, keep it until early fall, and then release it where they originally found it.*

Identification

easily recognized by the narrow, bright orange stripe running the length of the carapace.

B. Carapace quite rough; the rear marginals serrated; a definite keel or ridge runs the length of the carapace; one

keel through each of the costals, one through the center of the vertebrals; plastron reduced in size, usually white, faintly flecked with black; head heavy and unmarked; tail long, usually the length of the carapace.

Common snapping turtle (*Chelydra serpentina*), an aquatic species ranging over most of the United States.

(**Note:** Hatchlings of the alligator snapping turtle (*Macroclemys temmincki*) are sometimes offered for sale.

The snapping turtle, Chelydra serpentina, *is one of the most "prehistoric" appearing of the turtles, especially because of its large head, often heavily ridged and serrated shell, and the long tail with distinct crests. When cornered, snappers can inflict severe bites, and some have reportedly severed fingers. On the whole, snappers are good turtles to avoid, although they are easy to care for and almost invincible in captivity.*

Identification

They superficially resemble the hatchlings of the common snapper; however, the carapace is "squared off," pale brown in color, and the head has a definite hooked beak; the tail greatly exceeds the length of the carapace.)

5. **Carapace: Light to dark brown or black;** ovoid (elongated) in shape; head retracted straight back into the shell.

   A. Small in size, usually half the size of the red-ear; carapace faintly keeled in center of vertebrals and costals; plastron reduced in size, a) black with white spotting or b) reddish with black spotting; head large, lightly striped or plain.
      a) **Musk turtles** (*Sternotherus*, various species)
      b) **Mud turtles** (*Kinosternon*, various species).
      Some 14 species and subspecies of these aquatic turtles are found in the United States.

   B. Carapace light tan in color; a series of reddish "bumps" follow a line through the costals and vertebrals; plastron plain gray-white, usually not marked; head and legs heavily striped with very pale yellow.
      Spanish turtle (*Mauremys leprosa*), an aquatic species from northwestern Africa; often misrepresented as European pond turtle (*Emys orbicularis*).

   C. Carapace dark brown, sometimes black; a distinct keel running through the vertebrals and costals, the scutes between the keels sometimes presenting a sculptured, stippled appearance; plastron plain brown; head faintly marked with white; hind feet poorly webbed.
      Reeves' turtle (*Chinemys reevesi*), a marsh species from Japan.

   D. Carapace chocolate brown; distinctly keeled through vertebrals and costals; marginals edged with yellow; plastron without pattern; head heavy, with several broad white or yellow stripes, especially on the

Identification

chin; hind feet poorly webbed; usually seen at about 3 inches long.
Malayan pond or snail-eating turtle (*Malayemys subtrijuga*), a cold-sensitive tropical aquatic from southeastern Asia.

(**Note:** This turtle is extremely delicate in captivity, requiring skilled care and diet. Captives need at least some snails in the diet, as well as finely chopped raw shrimp in the shell, together with large amounts of calcium. A constant temperature in excess of 80°F is required to induce feeding.)

E. Carapace light to dark chocolate brown or black, sometimes with yellow or reddish centers in the large scutes; feet are poorly webbed. A prominent head patch of bright orange or yellow is present, sometimes divided individual patches of orange or yellow. Size is small, adults seldom over 3½ inches.
Bog turtle (*Clemmys muhlenbergi*), a rare

The stinkpot or musk turtle, Sternotherus odoratus, *is a very common eastern and central U.S. species that is very similar to the mud turtles but has a much smaller plastron. Baby stinkpots the size of a quarter or smaller are often abundant in early summer. The scent glands are well developed in this species and used at every opportunity.*

Identification

Spotted turtles, Clemmys guttata, *are the only eastern U.S. members of the genus still available as pets in most states (possession of both wood and bog turtles is prohibited in many areas). The juveniles have very few or even no spots on the shell and body, but large adults may be literally covered with small yellow spots. Because of the black color of the skin and shell, the spots stand out very distinctly. Adults are often partially terrestrial and feed on a variety of animals, from crayfishes to insects.*

Identification

species found in the sphagnum bogs and swamps in restricted areas in the northeastern United States. As a captive this species will not long survive unless provided with several highly specialized and difficult to maintain requirements, one of which is highly acid water.

(**Note:** Muhlenberg's turtle is more often collected than purchased. It is considered an endangered species by the International Union for Conservation of Nature, and a close watch is kept on those specimens that are housed in professional collections throughout the world. The animal cannot survive in areas where the habitat is radically altered by man, and it is suggested that unless specimens are found in an area about to be drained or bulldozed for development, they should be left where found and their presence reported to local wildlife agencies.)

F. Carapace dark bluish black. Feet poorly webbed; the entire carapace and head covered with bright yellow "polka dots" that vary greatly in density. Small size, adults seldom over 4 inches long.

Spotted turtle (*Clemmys guttata*), a hardy species from the eastern United States. Spotted turtles quickly become "tame," and in captivity they readily take food from the fingers. Proper care includes adequate swimming facilities plus considerable land areas allowing them to walk about a great deal.

G. Carapace light brown; heavily sculptured, usually with a distinctive mid-vertebral keel. Feet poorly webbed. The skin is usually bright orange or bright yellow, especially on the legs and neck.

Wood turtle (*Clemmys insculpta*), an essentially terrestrial turtle from the northern and northeastern United States. This beautiful turtle, when provided with proper care, probably makes the

73

Identification

finest pet of all the many species of turtles available. Once widely used as a food animal, it is now rare in some parts of its range, and many states afford it legal protection. One should familiarize oneself with local laws concerning this species before holding it captive. Often found in the same areas as eastern box turtles.

6. **Carapace: Light brown or black;** head withdrawn sidewise under the shell.

A. Entire animal colored light brown, black, or gray; plastron has a hinge near its broadest point, enabling the turtle to close the front of its shell; head rather broad, with a prominent flattened ear area.
  Gabon turtle (*Pelusios gabonensis*), a cold-sensitive, tropical aquatic from Africa. Hardy in captivity, often sold under the name of African mud turtle.

7. **Carapace: Pale tan or dark brown;** flat and circular in shape; soft and pliable at the edges; neck very long; a definitely tubular snout.

A. Carapace pale tan, sometimes lightly spotted or striped; plastron white or whitish gray; rear legs definitely paddle-shaped.
  Soft-shell turtles (*Trionyx* spp.), almost totally aquatic turtles found throughout eastern North America.

(**Note:** With the exception of the Florida soft-shell described under "B," hatchlings of the North American soft-shells look much alike to the untrained eye. Soft-shell turtles are also found throughout Africa and Asia, and hatchlings of these are sometimes offered for sale. All of these exotic species should be considered cold-sensitive and treated accordingly.)

B. Carapace heavily blotched in brown or black, edged with orange; plastron silvery gray, somewhat darker toward the rear; head and snout heavily marked with orange.
  Florida soft-shell turtle (*Trionyx ferox*), almost completely aquatic, from the Florida peninsula.

Identification

8. Carapace: High and domed; hind feet clublike or at least not fully webbed; head retracted straight back into shell.

A. Carapace brightly marked, orange on a brown ground or yellow on a black ground, occasionally plain horn-colored; plastron with a hinge, allowing the front and rear halves of the shell to close up. Forelegs heavily

Soft-shell turtles are preferred by many turtle keepers because they are such unusual turtles. All are almost totally aquatic, seldom leaving the water except to lay eggs. Few species bask like normal turtles. Their soft shells are very prone to injury in captivity from scrapping on rough surfaces, and injured soft-shells soon come down with fungus infections. Most species are also quite vicious and can inflict painful bites. Shown is the Florida soft-shell, Trionyx ferox.

scaled, usually orange or yellow. Males often have bright red eyes, females pale brown eyes. Usually sold as adults from 4 to 5 inches in carapace length.

Identification

Box turtles (*Terrapene* spp.), semi-terrestrial woodland to bog forms from North America. Six forms are known from the United States. The key fits those adults most commonly offered for sale: the eastern box turtle (*Terrapene c. carolina*), the ornate box turtle (*Terrapene o. ornata*), and the three-toed box turtle (*Terrapene c. triungis*).

Box turtles, Terrapene carolina *and* T. ornata, *are choice pet turtles and are still readily available in many states. They are often seen trying to cross roads in the spring and summer. Several states have decided that too many box turtles are being collected and have made possession of any box turtles illegal in the state. For this reason you must check your local laws before you pick up that next box turtle.*

Despite its name, the latter usually has four toes.

(**Note:** The eastern box turtle is protected by law in some areas, and local laws possibly concerning its possession should be checked before acquiring a specimen. The ornate box turtle requires a drier cage arrangement than the other two mentioned.)

B. Carapace strongly marked with a random black and yellow pattern, plastron pale yellow, occasionally splotched with black; hind feet clublike, usually with several heavy clawlike scales. The plastron is *not* hinged.

Identification

European tortoises (*Testudo* spp.), terrestrial forms from Europe and North Africa. The species most often offered for sale is Hermann's tortoise (*Testudo hermanni*) from Yugoslavia.

C. Carapace very dark brown or black; the scutes sometimes heavily striated or sculptured; plastron may be concave (hollowed out) with a projecting spur at the front (males); feet clublike and heavily scaled.

Gopher tortoises (*Gopherus* spp.), terrestrial forms from the semi-arid regions of North America; three species are found within the United States.

(**Note:** All are difficult to keep as pets. All are legally protected in the areas they inhabit, and one species, the Texas tortoise (*Gopherus berlandieri*), cannot be legally sold or possessed in the United States.)

Blanding's turtle, Emydoidea blandingi, *is a species of the Great Lakes and north-central U.S. In many ways it is like a box turtle, and it even has a hinge on the plastron. The bright yellow throat is distinctive, however. This species is poorly known and is quite local in distribution. In many areas where it was once common it is now absent or nearly so, for no apparent reason.*

Identification

D. Carapace very dark brown or black; the scutes sometimes heavily striated or sculptured, with a yellowish or horn-colored spot in the center of each shield. The plastron presents a "heavy" appearance, usually dull yellow in color and sometimes marked with black. The anterior edge is truncated (squared off), and the posterior edge may be notched.

South American tortoises (*Geochelone* spp.), terrestrial forms from the forests of South America. Two species are commonly sold as pets: 1) red-footed tortoise (*Geochelone carbonaria*), found throughout northern South America, east of the Andes. They require large amounts of drinking water and their humidity requirements are similar to those needed by our native box turtles. Young specimens quickly die if they are kept in dry, sandy terraria. The species is easily recognized by the heavy coral-red scales on the forelegs. 2) yellow-footed tortoise (*Geochelone denticulata*), easily recognized by the heavy yellow scales on the head and forelegs. In larger specimens the carapace tends to be definitely brownish in color, rather than black as in the case of the red-footed tortoise. The yellow-footed tortoise has a more extensive geographical range, and although young specimens require the same care as the red-footed tortoise, subadult and mature specimens prefer somewhat drier conditions.

Further Reading

Breen, J. F., 1974. *Encyclopedia of Reptiles and Amphibians.* T.F.H. Publ., Inc., Neptune, N.J.

Carr, A., 1952. *Handbook of Turtles,* Comstock Publishing Associates, New York, N.Y.

Conant, R., 1975. *A Field Guide to Reptiles and Amphibians of Eastern and Central North America,* Houghton-Mufflin Co., Boston, Mass.

Freiberg, M., 1981. *Turtles of South America.* T.F.H. Publ., Inc., Neptune, N.J.

Pope, C. H., 1949. *Turtles of the United States and Canada,* Knopf and Co., New York, N.Y.

Pritchard, P. C. H., 1979. *Encyclopedia of Turtles.* T.F.H. Publ., Inc., Neptune, N.J.

Schmidt, K. and Inger, F., 1967. *Living Reptiles of the World,* Hammish Hamilton Ltd., London.

Smith, H. M. and E. D. Brodie, Jr., 1982. *Reptiles of North America.* Western Publ. Co., Racine, Wisc.

Stebbins, R. C., 1966. *A Field Guide to Western Reptiles and Amphibians,* Houghton Mifflin Co., Boston, Mass.